La Fleur Qui Est
M.R.

Sogbe-Eden N'guessan

BookLeaf Publishing

Presentation by *BookLeaf Publishing*

Web: www.bookleafpub.com

E-mail: info@bookleafpub.com

ISBN: 9789358737400

First edition 2022

To my lovely M.R., I love you with all my might.

ACKNOWLEDGEMENT

I would like to acknowledge my sister Esh for introducing me to this platform, and providing me with the opportunity to share my experiences. I would also like to thank her for always sharing information about opportunities she knows I would benefit from.

I would like to acknowledge my husband for being a true partner and allowing me to explore all my interests without judgment.

I would love to thank doctors Shawki and Vernon for their support during and after the pregnancy. I would love to acknowledge doctors Miles, Elkin, Eckstein and Geronemus for maintaining check-ups and always reaching out with advice . I would also love to thank therapists Emily, Anita, and Cassandra for being extremely knowledgeable , friendly, giddy and caring.

Lastly, I would love to thank NYU Langone for providing us with legitimate care. Without this institution, I am not sure how great our experience would have been. and continue to be.

Foreign Feelings

It hit like a brick wall
Making it hard to comprehend,
Navigating life felt like such a haul
With no means to an end

This heightened sense of smell
Disturbed the general norm
To food, I waved farewell
To nausea with open arms

Sleep was my only ally,
Sacrificing daily activities;
To freedom I had to wave goodbye
This pregnancy kept me in captivity

Second Trimester

It brings me so much comfort
To embrace the idea of food
With no sign of revulsion
There is welcome of a happy mood

Immense bursts of energy
Allowing for longer walks,
Bringing back great memories
Of weights I used to chuck

Despite recuperation
No bowel movement in sight
I yearn for examination
But keep going on with all my might

The good outweighs the bad
With a gracious life ahead
Husband takes my heating pad
Patience hangs on by a thread.

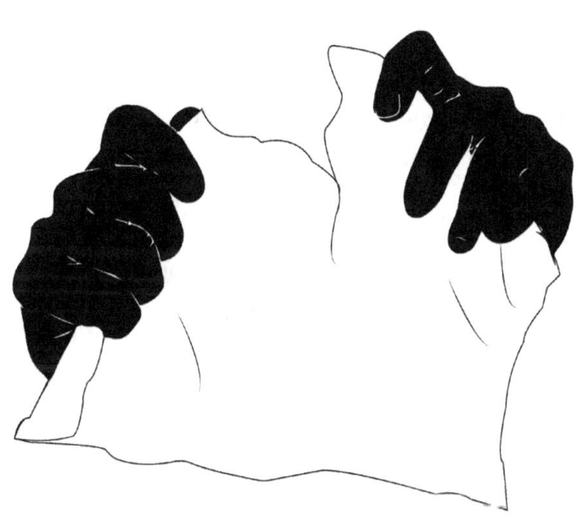

Third Trimester

Finally heading towards the homestretch
With some new symptoms to meet;
Baby's kicking way more, such a wretch,
It's showtime, "bring the heat"!

Braxton Hicks contractions make their debut,
Pausing all production for the day:
These are somewhat painful, who knew?
I hold on to a table, side-to-side I sway

Don't forget the intense back pain
As I thought things couldn't get worse
It intensified, over and over again
And in tears, I instantly burst

How dare the party proceed
Without this next feature
Sciatica then decides to impede
Oh, what a beautiful gesture

As a human petri dish
This is what I signed up for
To society, my traumas were dismissed
But to family, there were tears galore

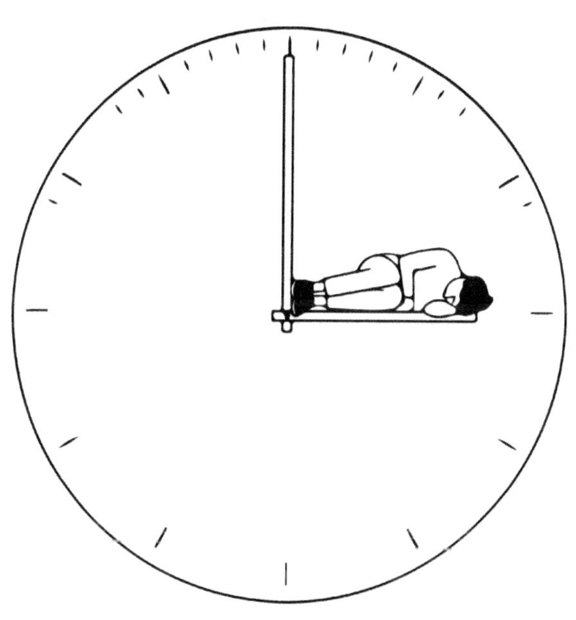

D-Day

Increased blood pressure
Caused induction to take place
I was excited for sure
Baby needed to hurry and show face

Induced contractions are intense
"Please inject me with that needle,
So the event can finally commence
as we make the baby's arrival"

Despite the intended numbing
All feelings were still endured
With continued medicine-pumping
I started to feel unsure

There is no going back now
This is D-Day, ready and fresh,
I pushed so hard, and screamed so loud
Here comes baby, in the flesh

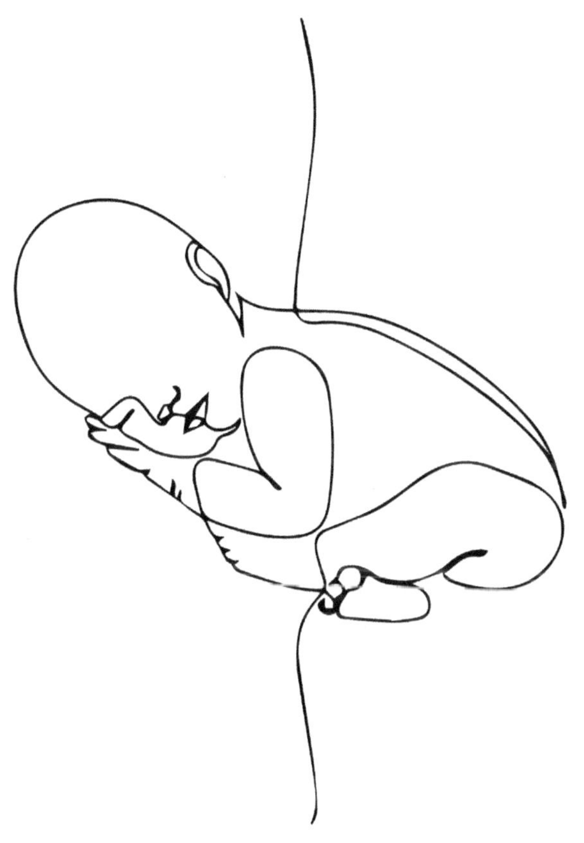

Bruising

Her first cry, warmed my heart,
First skin to skin, brought me joy
The real work, they said, "now it starts"
My mood was clearly destroyed

"There's bruising on the right side
This can happen with delivery"
Attentively I listen, while getting a ride
To the second floor for recovery

The bruising was bright red
But she looked so at peace
I couldn't stop smelling her head
Photos sent to my sister, of her niece

They were to conduct an MRI
To rule out certain conditions
I gladly gave her to them while my
Husband met up with the technicians

The News

The doctor enters the room,
With a sad look on her face
Giving us a feeling of doom
As she begins to pace

Finally, here comes the news
"Baby has Sturge-Weber Syndrome"
"I thought it was just a bruise"
"Unfortunately, that's not the outcome"

"80% of people with S.W.S
Will expect seizures to come
This might bring on a lot of stress"
With this news, my body went numb

No more words could penetrate
My body became hot
Shoulders equipped with instant weights
This was utterly, a lot!

Anxiety

New to the world,
So innocent and pure
My most precious pearl,
Has a condition with no cure

On edge, we were
Every second of the day
We felt for her
Yet, she was okay

Every movement, scrutinized
Every cooing, attended
Every look in her beautiful eyes
I knew on me, she depended

Any day, could be the day
But we let her be for now
Because as the doctors would say
There is nothing yet to sought out

The first time

This film was so funny
Until we noticed the shaking
Grabbing her hands, that were oh so chubby
My heart began aching

"Please, don't do this to me"
I cried with such force
Since life has no guarantee
I watched her with much remorse

Paramedics calmly tried
To say "Babies, seize at times"
The reason, I did not care to describe
When finally, my husband chimes

Medicine through I.V
Calmed the shaking arm
With an unsettled psyche
I tried drinking something warm

The Best Seat in the House

Treading up the thirteenth floor
With the amazing view of the Hudson,
Doctors came knocking on the door
Prepared to have a discussion

As told by the ones in charge,
Convulsions were on-going
The hole in my heart was large
As fear of losing her was growing

With this newfound confusion
Came a time of clarity
Then the feeling of seclusion
Followed by a sense of anxiety

Though, at such an ugly occasion
While she was snoozing about
Fireworks burst with explosion
Giving us the best seat in the house.

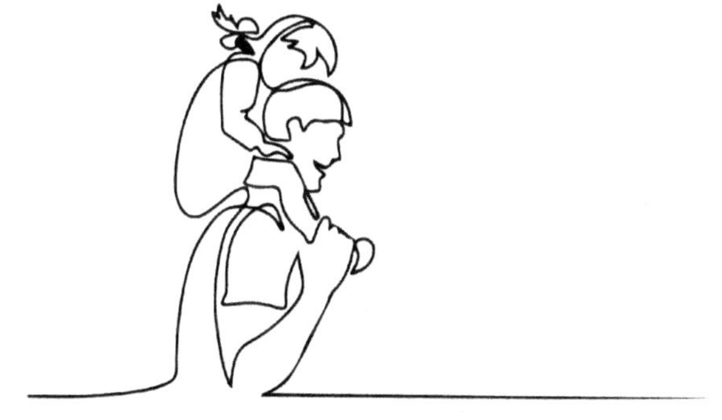

Anxiety- Part II

Baby's latest experience
Turned everything so serious
She followed along to the bathroom
Even when I was scheduled to join a Zoom

All hand movements, constantly observed
No action missed, so I always confirmed
Visitors, I shall not allow
To protect my child, I made a vow

Anxiety consumed me
To the highest degree
She needs to live her life as well
But right now, she's wrapped in my shell

"This S.W.S. is ruining my life"
I declare during this time of strife
I know, I ought to stop fussin'
As, my baby needs me, loosened.

The second time

Throwing up the medicine
Led to another episode
Constant stress that puts us in
Intensified my "mommy mode"

Now with emergency treatment
Within five minutes, they stopped
My mind officially went vacant
On the epileptic bandwagon we hopped

Two days later, another occurrence
Back to the E.R we went
Doctors continued with the assurance
Of nothing but continuous torment

Followed by two days overnight
Medication was increased
She had no choice but to fight
And I alongside, at least

Aftereffects

Convulsions brought weakness
The left side showed delays,
Doctor said "Please don't stress
One day she'll be doing relays"

Therapy was advised
Occupational and physical,
At least that, we recognized
Baby's life is never dull

Lots of appointments in our future
We shall go to, with a big smile
Our work schedules, we can maneuver
As we'll be doing therapy in style

Although aftereffects of the seizures
Hindered on-time development,
It'll get better, I am a believer
Give up on baby, we wouldn't

Development

Baby has become alert
Left arm and left leg move with grace
She's efficiently at work
And moving at her own pace

Three months passed
No seizure in sight
This may last,
Her future is bright

The clapping of hands,
The giggles about
To therapy, I thank
I have no more doubts

Mama

Month seven, still nothing
Forming teeth and babbling
Drools running down her chin
On her fingers, she starts sucking

The feet reach the mouth
"How amazingly flexible"
She bites her toes with the little sprouts
Evidence of stronger muscles

I witness the discovery
Of her newfound "choppas"
Then a word formed. Holy!
She just said the word "Mama"

Upset I couldn't record
I asked her to repeat
She smiled and was on board
The word, she went to speak

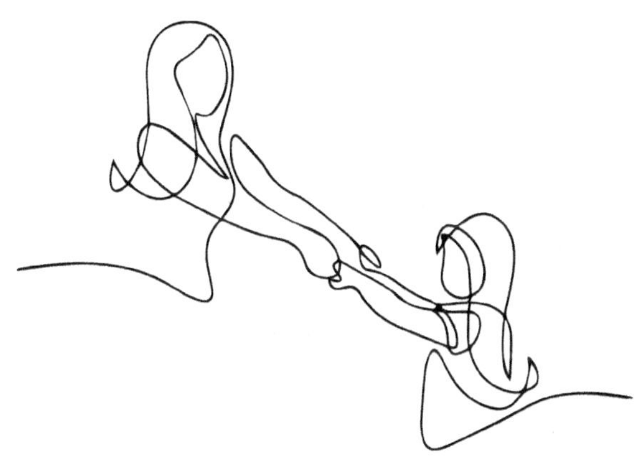

Teething

Not a one-shot deal
I wish we would've known
Down the hall, we hear the squeal
Very chilling to the bone

Put an end to this misery
But it must run its course
Distorted and bleary
Nature has no remorse

Choppers ripping through her gums
Would make anyone sore
This experience sort of sums
My lack of desire for anymore

Development- Part II

One smell of my food
And her mouth starts to water
As if she has enough teeth to chew
She instead reaches for a paper.

During feeding time, she grabs the spoon
Splattering it all over her clothes
She's independent, and very soon
She'll be scattering her barrettes and bows

We have no choice but to smile
As there is no ill intention
I can picture her running down an aisle
Of a store, in the toy section

Month 11, so close to her mark
once a newborn, now a toddler
next month, a candle we'll spark
she'll officially be 1 year older

Ode to M.R.

To you my dearest and most beloved
With smiles that brightens the world
The friendliest of all I've ever known
Hard to believe I have made this creation
With superpowers visible to the naked eye, of a
dynamic stain
Wavering with anger or hunger pains!
Throughout your lifetime,
There was much joyous remembrance

Nosiest of all
Your two pigtails flow about, from side to side
Dark brown, could be mistaken for black
As black as the one that beared you
You shall be tall, as you brush up on the big
ONE, with extended extremities
Pious of all
As you know nothing or intention
You, warm hearts, mine even more, as I sit here
and weep

The love is hard to explain
As it is one that will be forever aching
Chubby cheeks will eventually slim, my sweet
M.R.
You are my breath, and the reason I have risen

Struggles, you eat for breakfast, as I digest them
for supper
Continuously, you instruct me to depart from
precedents
Done, but not dusted, I leave you in your crib
alone to play
No more worries as we enter this new chapter of
our lifetime!

Open Book

Throughout this book
You've witnessed my experience
Some days, thoughts of being alone
Others, feeling gregarious

"Why me?" would cross my mind
However, I could not dwell,
These thoughts quickly put behind
Reclassified by her wonderful smell

This taught me perseverance
Followed by immense delight
True love felt, from the first appearance
Of the human, for whom I forever fight.